THOUGHTS OF AN INCARCERATED MIND

Dwn'Traquis Campbell

ISBN: 9780578892375

This Book Is Dedicated to My Loving Mother, Ruby Lee James: God bless your soul, Rest In Peace Mamma, I love you.

Table of Contents

Acknowledgments

I would first like to give my thanks and acknowledgments to God, for blessing me with a powerful mind and a special gift. Secondly, my beautiful and loving mother: I hope and pray that you are smiling down on me and also proud of me! I would like to thank all of my family and friends that played a part in the production of my work. I would especially like to thank my cousin, Brandon, for always being there and ready to believe in anything that I have set out to do. Thanks to my cousin, Polly, for loving me when I had nobody; thanks for taking those long drives to come and love me when I had lost my mom and was at my lowest. Also, thanks to Buddy Boi, my friend and my brother, for all that you do and have done. Lastly, I would like to thank the many prison staff and correctional officers that have helped break me down to the point where I had to turn to God. Thanks for making me see who I really am, thanks for letting me make my light shine, thanks for giving me my voice, and thanks for your part in my struggle.

Introduction

I started writing poetry when I was maybe twelve or thirteen years old. People have always told that I had a way with words, but I've never been a good speaker in front of crowds. I believe that came from lack of self-confidence; I never thought that any of what I did or said was ever good enough.

I was full of doubt when I started this book. I think that everyone in this world needs positive support; we all need something or someone to tell us that we're doing a good job and to not give up. Those words alone have the potential to push a person to take the extra step they may need in order to succeed or reach their goals. One of the reasons that I fell in love with poetry is because of the fact that it doesn't have to be pretty or sound just right. Poetry is a form of art and self-expressions that touches the people who needed to hear those words the most. It's amazing to see how many people that you never knew felt the same exact way that you felt but just couldn't find the right words to describe it. My only wish is that my words and my work will help a soul in need, hopefully my words can motivate and inspire you to be great and to never give up!!.

Sounds of Injustice

Sounds of injustice is sometimes five years of hell sometimes even life. Take a boy away from home, throw him in a jungle of inhumane, and expect him to come out right. Where is the justice in that? Crackers creating laws every day to make sure it stays that way, and they still getting away with that taught us what they wanted us to know; take away our fathers just to stagnate our growth, then smile in our faces like a nigga don't know, gave us welfare and food stamps so we'll just shut up and go, and paid off black politicians to play like they ain't know, sounds of injustice. They came up with a dozen more ways to kill a nigga. Took the away ropes, gave a black man a robe and said, "let that nigger kill that nigger, then they try to tell good black folks that they are getting ahead." Try to convince them that the ones living in poverty they deserve to be dead, where is our 40 acres and that mule you promised? Worked our ancestors to death and we still left nothing and them crackers created extortion. So, where the fuck is our justice. We still screaming and marching for peace, and them white police still bussing they assassinated Brother Malcolm, then give us Al Sharpton and Rev. Jackson then blinded us all with Jordan's, gold chains and Michael Jackson. Yea, I admit that y'all got us. We were dirt poor until that white man gave niggas all that powder, then crack came along and had us killing for fake power, every time our eyes open they try and find a way to close it, and get rid of ever black man that try his best to expose it, there's no justice when injustice. So, it's time we let them know it, don't just talk about justice muthafucka show it, sounds of injustice......

Fresh In The System

December 23,2001.

Two days before Christmas and once again I was kicked out of my mother's house. It was cold and I had not been to sleep in two days. The few hours I did sleep I was bunched up in the back seat of my friend's car; me and three more of my good brothers shared that Smoke Grey Delta 88 like it was a home.

Sad thing was, out of us all I was the only fool that was able to go home, but I had chosen my friends and the cold streets over my family and a warm home. Back then I could not have told you why I made that choice, but now I can. Even though family is blood, they're your kinfolk, you grow up together, eat together, and sleep together, but the truth is that family is the ones who love you and show you they love you. Love is an action. So, at that time in my life those guy's and those cold streets were my family, that is who I felt love from, that's who I ate with, and that's who I slept in empty trailers and cold cars with. I remember that night so clearly, I remember being hungry, and angry, I remember three guys I knew from the trailer park I was staying in pull up in a pretty, burgundy Monte Carlo. They were cool dude's, I guess. They jumped out of the car, with the music blasting, Pastor Troy booming through the speakers. The one who I was most cool with called me to the side while the other two talked it up with my other brothers. Dude began telling me that he had a lick for us (A Robbery). Then he pulled out a gun, at the time I did not know what kind of gun it was, but my eyes got big as two quarters. Seeing that gun, I know now that he knew he had me from the look in my eyes, I was sold." Yea I'm down" Was the words out of my mouth. He smiled at me and gave me dap, "I knew you was a real nigga" was the words he used to fully rill me in. Being so called "real" is the goal growing up in the urban community. He turned and headed for the car, with me on his heals, and the rest followed. My brothers standing around the ole trusty Delta 88 screamed in concern. "Shaad where the hell you are going man?" with concern for a friend in their voice. "I'll be back Bra" I yelled back. My friend Ced ran up to the car, holding the car for, looked me in the eyes, and said "Bra get yo ass out this car." I sat there in the front seat feeling like the realist Nigga alive and told my friend "I got this, fall back." His words to me with him shaking his head were, "Stupid ass Nigga." We drove off with that Pastor Troy booming Visa Verse, and I felt so free trying to live a life that wasn't meant for me. Later during that drive, I found out that it wasn't a lick, that we were out doing freelance robberies, that would eventually lead me to doing ten years in the Georgia Dept of Corrections. During those ten years I continued to be a follower, I continued to let myself and my mind be manipulated by others. I continued to misinterpret foes as friends. Back then I did not see it, because I was not able to step away from myself and see myself. In other words, I wasn't able to see and reflect. Ten years later I walked out of prison worse than when I went in.

100 years

100 years ago, they seen peasants and we were Kings.

Sad to say one hundred years later we are experiencing some of the same things.

100 hundred years ago they gave a little and took a lot

Black men and women humiliated, tortured treated like things we not.

Can you picture one hundred slaves, one hundred whips on their backs?

And 100 years later my brothers and sisters are still under attack.

For hundreds of years, hundreds of Black men have been degraded, replaced slave owners with the police, changed laws to keep us Incarcerated.

One hundred years one hundred tears in a bucket,

Been fucked over and abused so long that we all have said just fuck it.

We're a people that comes from generations of Malcom X's and Harriett Tubman's,

From not being able to read, not allowed in schools to having our own universities.

One hundred years ago jazz took over the Harlem nights,

100 years later how we lose sight of our true fight?

One hundred years ago we weren't ok with what they allowed us to have,

300 years of oppression and niggas screaming let the past be the past.

100 years ago, some of our ancestors were in their primes,

Now take a minute to picture what they went through, and judge that by what we're going through now.

100 Years

Incarceration

Being incarcerated is like being an "Adult Child."

Like being grown and a 10-year-old at the same time.

It's almost like being on punishment for years at a time.

Most of the poems I write about being in prison hold a lot of anger and resentment.

I think I have always tried to take responsibility for my actions, but that doesn't mean I can't be angry while doing so.

As of today, I have given the prison system almost 13 years of my life and I am only 33 years old.

Prison is full of fake happiness; a sane person could never be happy here.

Everything that makes you smile finds a way to make you cry.

I think the worst of it all is being trapped around so many good brothers who have lost hope.

Sometimes, hope and prayer is all a person has when you lose yourself.

Prison or Slavery,
Slavery or Prison?

I got to wake up when they say wake up, just like my ancestors,

I got to work when that tell me to work,

I was brought here by force in their chains and shackles,

I was sold,

Only this time sold out,

On the way here, some others were murdered and killed,

Some were beat, some have wounds and scares that will never heal.

Talked to with disrespect and hate by that young white boy that is afraid of not just me but who I am, just like my ancestors,

Being beat by five white officers that cannot beat you alone by yourself, just like my ancestors,

Then we can't forget them house niggas, the black officers that watch and see the injustice done to their own kind, and they won't say anything or try to stop it, and have the nerve to be upset when they hear that their brother, father or cousin was beat by the police, they dress us how they want us to dress,

Tell us when we can see our family and kids, just like my ancestors,

So y'all tell me what is the difference in the two?

Walls, Bars and Concrete

Trapped inside of these four walls, buried deep within the bars of my confinement, surrounded by concrete. The walls capture my thoughts trying their hardest to enable them to think outside of my mental captivity. These bars taking away my physical freedom and the concrete constantly reminding me, creating a barrier between me and what I yearn. If these walls could speak and tell the tales of the hurt and the pain that exists so vividly within the souls of the men and women behind these bars, or show the chokehold that's on the ones who have no choice but to submit to the concrete, the walls are stained with dreadful memories, the bars continuously tainting our thoughts, while our souls fall victim and drown in the concrete.

Imprisoned

One of the hardest things about being imprisoned, enslaved, locked away? Is knowing that you left your Loved ones out there to try and live life happily without you there.

While you lay in bed all day forcing yourself to sleep, just so the day can be another day imprisoned.

Behind these fences and walls

Behind these fences man everybody
plotting, and everybody scheming,

You are tormented daily realizing there isn't
no escaping, and those walls cannot be
moved physically,

at war with yourself, them, whoever else
and millions of demons

Secluded to a world where you have no one
else, nobody but you, I, me, and myself.

Most times you do not know who to believe,
what to believe or who to trust,

Yea I know it's crazy, so we learn how not to
trust, and learn how to believe, not what
you hear them say but what you can see.

Behind these fences, all things have a
motive, days and weeks are related,
mentally overrated, whoever tells you
differently believe me they're crazy.

The best minds have fallen victim to
believing that it is over,
mentally defeated to what is really a
spiritual struggle,
Once these walls take your soul, that is
when you really become a lost brother.
These fences don't love no man,
these walls are put here to break you,
Stay strong through your struggle and do
not let these fences and walls take you.
Behind these fences and walls

Prison Nowadays

Prison Nowadays looks so appealing, kids, mostly black look at prison and think "Man, I can do time with no problem." Then when they get inside, they meet a new reality. You may have a killer mentality but have you ever been around two hundred angry men and all of them have a kill or be killed mentality? I've watched many tough gang bangers barricade themselves inside of a room, and watch their fellow brothers as they were murdered in cold blood. I watched dead bodies lay stiff for hours before any officer decided to come in and move them, I watched dudes walk around and eat cup soups like they had no problem in the world with eating around the horrific scenes. A word of advice for the youth, never be quick to follow in someone's footsteps that has never been through or witnessed any of the things that he asks of you, my sole purpose for writing this book was to give some enlightenment on the system that many black men glorify, I'm doing my share hoping that I can change at least one life and save at least one kid from going through and seeing the things I've seen and been through. I pray that our young Black Men can start to appreciate and value their lives more, start to value their families more, start to value their freedom more, and finally understand that our kids and families needs us more than prison need us, be different.

Captivity

You may have my body; unwillingly but that's

the only part of me that you will ever get

My mind travel places that you could never

phantom, without boundaries and beyond

measures. Your chains and shackles are only

but so good, your words and your thoughts go

without meaning. I was once so consumed,

living in your world of criticism and negativity;

the more I fought for a worthless freedom the

more your world befriended me, I finally

realized that for so long I allowed you to dwell

inside of my mind, I allowed you to reside in my

soul, I let you dictate my peace, and let your

words and thoughts of me reach the vessels of

my heart which made me truly a captive.

Now that I know and am no longer blinded you

seem so upset, so upset that now I see your

hatred at my growth, it angers you to see that I

have found the keys which I have possessed

since the birth of a king, the keys which is the

knowledge of self, wisdom and the power to

overcome your oppression. I became a force

when I was able to unlock the Vault where my

mind was secured, I became different when I

learned that captivity isn't just a place but a

mindset.

Murder

March 8, 2015.

By this time, I had been out of prison around three and a half years. Yet and still walking, talking, and acting as if I didn't spend ten years of my life in prison. I had a two-year-old son. By now I had a mother who was not doing good health wise. I had every reason in the world to do better than what I was doing. But I chose the other route. I chose to run the streets and gang bang better than I ever have. I put my mind and heart into being the best Gangster that I can be. I shot my guns for fun. I took lives, and hurt people for nothing, just a sad human. I was a bad excuse for a Black man. I was a bad example. Once again on this night, I left the house where my son was sleeping, jumped back into another car, with another group of friends, only to end up headed to prison once again. This night I felt wrong, I felt it tugging at my heart, I felt that this was not a ride that I really wanted to take. And once again this time around I loved my friends more than I loved my family. And even now my loyalty is my loyalty. That night once again I let my judgement be manipulated, and my mind. After hurting people for so long and getting away with it, that day was my day. And that night I took a man's life. I took a son from his mother, and a father from his children. Yet and still, I didn't feel any different. I thought after killing a man in front of dozens of people that my heart would feel different, that my soul would feel different. But I felt the same. That night laying in my bed, looking into my son's eyes, I asked God was I the devil? Not knowing what to do or where to go, I did what any scared man would do, and ran.

Blood on Your Hands

"It's blood on our hands, from the life of another man. The blood of another man has left a stain on my hands,

It's blood on my hands, even after all these good deeds yet it's still blood on my hands, after all of the forgiveness, still it's blood on my hands."

Before my time at Lee County Corrections in South Carolina, I had been to some fucked up places, like Hayes State prison, Reidsville, and Smith State Prison, all in Georgia. Man lemme tell you, I thought those places was the worse of the worse, but not until I landed at Lee County did I really see a different type of prison, it was like an all-male college campus, we did what we wanted when we wanted, I had did a ten year stretch in Georgia so I knew the do's and don'ts of prison. I knew that I would fight for my rights and respect as a man, so walking from the intake building I can't lie, I was confident but I still had some anxiety, so I turned that three minute walk into a five just to get myself together, after all, It wasn't like I was happy to be there. It's just that I thought I wouldn't see the inside of a prison again, and there I was walking into that concrete jungle once again, gearing myself up for battle, preparing myself for war, making sure that no matter what happened that I make it home, that I make it out. The officer that was escorting me must've been doing his job a while because I think he slowed down too just to allow me to start to adjust as quickly as possible. We finally arrived at the dormitory that I was placed in, same prison look, big and creepy like, even for a grown man, pulling up to any prison gives you that feeling, like pulling up into a gladiator arena, before we could pull open the door I was hit with a huge contact, and I'm not talking about no Reggie I'm talking about that loud pack, and I said to myself my current drug free life would no longer be drug free, walking through the halls that led to the dorm I was in awe as we passed by many different groups of guys that were talking and starring. I could see that each one of them and myself were doing the exact same thing and that was sending each other's faces through our own database, making sure the next man wasn't an enemy or a foe; and it's really like that, your first rule of entering any place is to learn and know your environment. So as I strolled through the front door of the dorm, I strolled in with my shoulders high, head high, heart on full. It's already crazy coming in with ten different people, but coming in by yourself, all eyes on me, quiet, more faces analyzing me, no laughs no smile, just animosity and tension mixed with three or four different drugs in the air. I stood there for a second looking around trying to locate the room number I was assigned to. After a few seconds I saw it and headed over to the door, even though I was assigned to the room I knew one thing that you always do and that is knock before you enter any prison cell, that's a quick way to get yourself stabbed. It's not too much an inmate can really have control over, and a few of the things they can is simple as their cell door, or the light switch that could get a man beat to sleep. After standing there knocking for a full minute, one of the shortest inmates I ever saw swung open the door looking at me like he was ready to strike. I'm looking down on him like don't do it L'il Man, he like, "Yea what's up!" With a voice full of aggression. I wasn't expecting his voice to be so deep, but I could tell he was trying to make it sound that way, which was kind of funny at the moment. But that l'il short ass inmate had informed me that two people was already in that room and I had to find somewhere else to go, cool with me I had already been hip to that type of shit–one thing I would never do is bunk with a person I can't vibe with. I will not close my eyes around a person I can't trust or don't trust or just don't know. That l'il inmate became one of my good brothers, Butta G was his name. Then one of my favorite brothers in South Carolina walked up on me, he told me later that I looked like I was one of his brothers, but yea his name L'il D, I remember him walking up on me like," What's good witcha bra you part of anything? "My Shorty had tried to get me to promise her that I would let that life go, but she doesn't understand the importance of brotherhood and Loyalty, loyalty defines a man because what your loyal to says a lot about the person you are, so I tell L'il D that I'm Growth and Development with my chest all out. He smiles, happy at the fact of how good he is at recognizing one of his own, he grabbed my mat and led the way. He explained to me quick that shit was dangerous and could go stupid at any time so always be on yo shit. I used my two ears at what they're best at and listened. On the way to my new room to meet my new roommate, L'il D only told me one thing that stood out, and that was "Yea G, bra you moving in the room with good people, but he crazy!" In my mind I'm thinking like, what the fuck you mean he good people but he crazy? It's so many different types of crazy in the world, but crazy in prison is a different type of crazy, so I was on my P's and Q's bout this nigga. This was the day that I met one of the craziest niggas I ever met, with a name like Zilla what can you expect? My second day there the police shut the air off and shot cannisters of Mace and pepper spray into the dorm, for no real reason at all. I remember being in that cell and it was just so much of this stuff in the air that the entire dorm was coughing and gasping for air, all two hundred inmates. I didn't want to panic or seem like I was panicking but I got to tell you, I think I'm a tad bit claustrophobic, because man when I can't breathe a little bit I get to bugging out, and I was trying to hold that shit in. But Bra must've seen it in my eyes, man I don't care what y'all thinking about me, but them dirty ass cop had cut the water off. I couldn't believe it! I looked at my roommate and I asked him with every serious bone in my body, "Are they trying to kill us?" He laughed at me, it's funny now, but that furthermore made me realize that yea this dude was crazy and this damn Lee County was crazy, but my roommate being the good guy that he is helped me out by dipping a towel into the toilet and wrapping that towel around my face. I could breathe a bit better, but I was like damn man where the heck they put me at? This was like some stuff from overseas, I really don't care to go too far into everything that took place at Lee County. I don't want to go through having to change names or groups while explaining to y'all one of the worst experiences I've had in prison. In April of 2017, one of the most deadliest riots in US history took place at Lee County Corrections. More than half a dozen men lost their lives; like I said before I grew up around violence, I lived in violence, I served time in the most violent prisons, but never before had I seen that many people get killed in one place. In one small area of the world in such violent ways, shootings and stabbings are so much more different, shooting is usually far off, or a couple feet away while stabbing a person is so up close and personal, so heated. I think a lot of people stopped talking for like a hour, it was only silence and killing, with death in the air, I didn't know what to think of it, I didn't know everything that was going on. All I know was that I was told to suit up get right get my weapons and stand firm, so there I was with my life on the line standing for what I believed in and who I love. One black man lost his life in the dorm I was in that day, but throughout the yard it was many more that lost their life, Rest In Peace to them brothers. The facility had been taken over by the inmates for more than eight hours, when the National Guard showed up with Ak's and automatic weapons to assist the officers with locking the doors and rounding up the wounded; and it was plenty wounded somewhere around twenty three inmates had been wounded during that riot, just that fast it could've been you with blood on your hands. One of the best things about freedom is the ability to move, the ability to create your own space, might not seem like much to some people, but it means a lot.

What's Missing?

Love is the first law of the land, it's the foundation for everything, without love most of us wouldn't be here, everything grows better with love. So I think that's one of the major things that's missing in today's community, seems like everyone has that "it isn't me or my people that it happened to" attitude. I feel like it's almost a fact that the black and urban communities are not as together as we once we're when it comes to our kids. I'm only thirty five and even when I was growing up it was certain things I would not do or say around another adult, because they could've checked me, then took me to my momma and I would get my butt tore up. But it's like parents now and days just saying, "That isn't my kid," and, watch a kid that could any day be any one of ours do something that we know we wouldn't let our kids do in front of us. Don't matter if it isn't your kid or your friend kid, it's OUR kid, so it's our responsibility, not to act as the parent, but to act out of love. Because at the end of the day, you would love and appreciate any person that saved your son's life, or stopped him from catching twenty five years in prison, Right? Every day I talk to real life gangsters, real life killers and you wouldn't believe how many actually voice out loud that they hate it, they hate what they did, they hated the way they treated people, hated the crime they committed, they hate the situation they're in, they hate that they didn't listen. Real talk. I've heard hundreds of grown men confess how much they wish they would've listened to their mom or dad, or friend or girlfriend. It's always that story of, "Man my such and such told me don't take my ass over there with them people," or, "My mama told me to leave that dude alone." We all got that story, we all got that somebody that told us not to do it, so whether that kid decided to listen to you or not, still show your love to your community by saying something. Without love we surely would not have made it this far, so we must give what we have received. I wanted my first book to be the book to introduce me to the world as an inspiration, so that not I by myself can be great, but to also do my share and my responsibility. I also learned that race not racism will always be present in all situations. I didn't say race would play a part, but race will be present, only the individuals involved have control over if it plays a part or not, but what team, or race, country, or species don't want to see someone like them win? It is natural for a person to want to see something or someone that's like you or look like you win, why? Because you can Envision yourself doing that same thing or something better, when it's someone doing it that looks like you or come from where you come from, so that mean don't be afraid to want, and help someone like you do something right, don't be afraid to be the kid that helps another kid do the right thing. If you meet someone that tells you prison is fun, get away from them the fast way, they don't mean themselves no good let alone you, prison is like waking up on punishment every day, and you can only go to the kitchen and to the bathroom, imagine that young one, imagine your mama and the police telling you that you can't leave your house for the next five years, and the police guarding the house so you can't leave, you just stuck from your room to the kitchen to the bathroom? Think about that for real, and to add insult to it, they only let you take one shower a week, and they choose all the food that you eat, and when you can eat it? Imagine that: imagine being sixteen years old locked in a warehouse with two hundred grown men, one hundred murderers, one hundred gang members, one hundred men that probably never see freedom again–one hundred men that don't care about living or dying, and one hundred men too dumb to know the difference. Imagine what kind of person you would have to be or become to survive? Everything or person cannot adapt to its environment, some flowers can grow in snow, but too much water will kill them. So, understand that some gangster's and killers that you grew up around, or think you may be, or who you may be like, don't always adapt to the prison environment, yes, I'm trying to scare you and yes everything that I'm saying to you is one hundred percent real and factual.

Black Lives Matter

We pledged to allegiance to the flag of someone else's United States of America. We knew for way too long how General Lee finessed us.

Forced our ancestors to fight and die for things in which they didn't believe in.

Our Black Men out there dying and being wounded for a country that they wasn't even safe in.

White man got a dollar, Black Man got a dollar and they both look exactly the same,

But that Black Man's dollar can't go to the same place or couldn't create the same change.

They told them that they would go to hell if they didn't pick that cotton,

Now they throw us in jail for nothing, and kill our youngsters dead for jogging,

Deny us our rights and take what they want with no warnings.

Brother's running away and still get shot, who is they protecting, please tell me who are they serving?

We don't want your pity, we only demanding equality,

Now the last are first and you all are slowly becoming the minority.

War or peace we all want the latter,

We will not continue to scream it anymore we will Show you that All Black Lives Matter.

Self-Genocide

When will we wake up and smell the oppressors coffee?

Why do we continue to sleep through what we see so clearly?

Turning a blind eye to the bullshit that we see so vividly.

How do we constantly accept all the wrongs in the mist of our rights?

While we put on a display of all the things that we've had to endure for all of our life.

Not only are we killing each other's body we're also destroying each other's minds.

How do we tear down everything that our ancestors have died for?

We show them constantly that their work, blood, sweat and tears were in vain,

Us alone makes a nation of scholars look insane.

We speak of love but our actions show otherwise, we destroy our brother's Hopes and also killing them on the inside,

We're losing our sense of direction losing hope, and we continue to put aside our pride,

We are the definition of a self-genocide.

What It Takes

It's a few things that I think it actually takes to ensure that our children make it in today's society, and one of them is Education. In order for us to do we must know, whatever the dream is, we must all commit to his or her dream. Another one is discipline, once we have committed, we should all stand firm on the commitment. I think discipline speaks for a lot in itself. Us adults understand now how much a lack of discipline has hurt us growing up. We remember all the times that we gave up, we remember all the times the people around us allowed us to quit, when most times all we needed to be great was just that a small tiny push, and boom you got a great and successful example. I remember quitting a lot growing up, and being allowed to quit, quitting is not good for any kid, young child, or a teenager, it's not good for character, it's not good for the mindset, sometimes you can do really bad at something, or not be enjoying doing it, but you still take away something important or something of value that could be helpful to you later on in life. A lot of us have quit a lot early in life, then it grows with us and we turn into an adult quitter going from job to job, house to house, apartment to apartment, partner to partner, college to college, and major to major. I believe that the greatest ones are the ones who didn't quit, the ones who had that extra little push that they may have needed or that inspired them, that one person in their life who said, "Hell No You Not Quitting." As kids growing up, we all have wanted to make our parents and the elders in our life proud. As parents, guardians, and elders we got to show interest in what they got going on. What kid would care if nobody in his/her life don't care? When you have kids, nieces and nephews, young ones in the neighborhood, that's what should come first, because I can almost guarantee kids always do their best when there's someone they love, respect or look up to in attendance. So, I'm feeling like people are saying to themselves like dude who are you, some kind of disciple or something like that? Yes lol...But for real though, be real right now and think back, don't matter what you do for work, what school you go to, don't matter how much money you make, think back to when you were 10 years old, think about something you were doing, or where you were, do that for two minutes........ Okay I'm back, now for two minutes think about when you were 12 years old, try to remember a class you took in school, a sport you played, a program you attended...... Okay I'm back, and the reason I asked the reader to do that quick thinking exercise is to show that the things we do and the decisions we make at the age of ten and the ages of twelve are very much important and special to us because we remember them. Some of us remember a lot of them, and I am not the one to judge. So, I'm not going to ask anyone how they feel about the things they just remembered, because the reader knows, and they can choose to tell whom they want. But all in all, I say that it is very important to establish the proper amount of love and discipline and commitment at those early ages.

Okay, one more for the people who still feel like I am just running my mouth about something I don't know nothing about. For one minute right now just think back to the one person who you had in your life growing up that you know absolutely would not let you quit something that they knew that you loved doing......Okay I'm back, and the answer to that question is if you're doing what you love to do, or around it or in the area of it you are one of the ones who had someone in their life that absolutely wouldn't allow you to just quit something you love to do–not just because you we're afraid of them, rather you just knew this wasn't the person you wanted to tell no non sense about quitting, and mostly because you see how much they cared that you cared and the last thing you wanted to do was disappoint them. Some people may have had a person in their life like, but something happened, they either died, or moved away, get locked up, those things can happen to any of us. The Love and

Discipline process is a reaction that should be passed down from generation to generation, not quitting not allowing us to quit and not accepting quitting.

So I think what it takes is a nice mixture of people to grow great roots that will develop strong branches that will develop stronger branches that will develop stronger branches that will develop stronger branches and so forth and so on. Because at the end of the day, you have to be a fool if you would say that right now if you are not happy or successful and content with where you are or what you're doing in life, that you wouldn't if you could go back and change the things you may have done when you we're a young preteen or a young teenager. If being successful, or being something great for yourself, or feeling prideful that what you are or who you are is important to someone else is not meaningful to you, you will not begin to understand any of what I'm speaking on. Even as adults, most people still enjoy hearing someone tell you truthfully that, "Hey I'm really proud of you," or "Hey you're really doing a great job," or "Hey we all just wanted to say you're doing a great job at life right now keep up the good work."

Note to the Young Brothers on the Ropes

Being different might seem lame right now, being successful might seem like you aren't built like that, but when you really grow up you will thank God and thank yourself for making the right decisions in life. Don't end up throwing your life away just to prove yourself to a bunch of people that's not going to write you or come visit you when you end up in somebody's prison, I'm all for my Black community so I got to do my part and inform you young brothers. So, to all you smart, intelligent and strong black men do something different, be different. Make your family proud of you. Prisons are being built and they're making room for the new shipment of young black men. Please don't be a part of that bus ride! Every day I see and talk to black men in their twenties and thirties that will never know what it's like to be a free man again and I promise you nearly all of them will take back whatever it is that they have done. When you're getting old and your mother is getting old and your kids are growing up without you there it's going to take a chunk out of your heart and soul, so please young black man be a leader, set trends, and be different.

Separation

After my first couple years in prison, I realized how serious the separation from my family and friends were; it seemed like everyone just expected that I was okay or just didn't care, that's what prison do to black families, prison for us is like the military to other families, it's almost like most of our family expect and accept that at least six out of ten black men in their family will go to jail or prison once in their life. Outside of my mom and my brother I never received letters or visit from any other family members while incarcerated on my first bid. I received ten years for two robberies that I committed at sixteen years old, I was a first-time youthful offender, no priors no arrest record and I still did all ten years. My mom came to see me every weekend and wrote me at least twice a week, she would cry every visit, she would always say that she wished she could change places with me, she was the only one that really saw what the prison system had done to me; she saw how my behavior changed, she saw how my smile wasn't the same anymore, and I saw the hurt and disappointment in her eyes. After five years inside I was completely institutionalized, I didn't think about the streets it started to seem like time had stopped, I was completely separated from everything I had known about the streets, all I thought about was what I was going to do the next day in prison. My high school sweetheart had left me after a couple of years and I didn't blame her, I had pushed her away, from the things I was seeing and being involved in I didn't know if I would make it back home to her, I was separated. Prison had overpowered my mind and my ability to think as a free man, and at that time I didn't know that I controlled my sense of freedom. I spent my days running around the penitentiary playing games, I didn't get an education I didn't learn anything but how to be a better criminal, I was separated. What really did me in was when I didn't hear from my mother for almost four years, picture being twenty years old, in prison and all you had was your mom, and your mom would write to you and visit you every week no matter what, and then out of nowhere you don't hear from her or see her for nearly four years. That's the thing that nearly drove me crazy. I attempted to take my life three times in those four years–I was so hurt, so lost that I was separated, that was when my time really got hard for me. I didn't know what was wrong or where my mom was, I didn't know if she had given up on me or if she was okay. I had no way to call her no number, no address to write to her, she was all I had in the world and without her I was truly separated. I gave up hope, and there's nothing harder to look at than a man that has given up hope. After that I ended up spending close to two years in isolation, I would go days without eating, I took pills that wasn't mine, I cut my arm numerous of times, I tried hanging myself, and what hurt the most out of all that is the only attention I got was from the four walls inside of that cell. They would take me to medical and take care of my wounds give me a bandage then throw me back in that cell with nothing, no mattress no running water no books no nothing, just me and the thoughts that I was running away from, I was separated. I remember the happiest and saddest day I ever experienced while doing that first bid, it was the first time in my life that I went from being one hundred percent happy to being so sad and hurt. I was laying in my bed daydreaming about food, I was so hungry. It was a Saturday and they only fed us twice on the weekends, so I'm lying there and my stomach is touching my back, then the police come to my door and says, "Campbell visitation." I heard the words but I didn't believe them, my heart didn't believe them; it had been almost five years since anyone had come to visit me, it had been almost five years since I had received a letter from anyone. The officer knocked again, "Campbell get ready I'll be back to get you in five minutes." I jumped up out of my bed and I was shaking with emotions. I was wondering who had come to see me. I hurried and got dressed in less than three minutes and was banging on the door yelling to the officer I'm ready after four minutes, all I could think about was a candy bar and a bag of chips and just to see someone and talk to someone that knew the real me, and that loved me. I had been so separated, the officer finally came and got me and escorted me to the visitation room. When we reached the room where visits were held I could see through the glass, I started searching the room with my eyes, then I saw my brother and his kids and my face was filled with the biggest smile ever. Then I saw my beautiful mother, the mother I hadn't seen in almost five years. But slowly my smile started to fade, something wasn't right, she wasn't the same; she was smaller, and looked older, as I got closer to the table where they were, I saw a walker. Then when I got to the table and started to hug her, I noticed that she couldn't move her right arm. I held her, and she cried in my arms and told me how sorry she was. I found out that day that my beautiful mother had suffered from at least six strokes back to back and had paralyzed her body on the right side. I was devastated, I was crushed, my appetite was gone, my heart was broken, all the times I had daydreamed of all the things that me and my mom would do when I got home was broken into pieces. I still ate good that day after hearing her reassure me several times that she was okay and that she was doing rehab therapy getting herself back together. I left that visitation room that day feeling worse than when I went, seeing her like that had taken something away from me–it took some caring away from me and chipped away at my heart and soul, I was surely separated.

You never know
who you may need

I was living in Alabama, after I moved there from Georgia. I got to Alabama thinking it was super slow and country. Then boom... I find out things are real in Alabama. So, dudes from Alabama be beefing with the dudes from Georgia. I'm cooling with the dudes from Bama end up getting shot at the fair in Georgia, by the dudes from Georgia. We finally catch one of the dudes I know from Georgia. Bra ain't have nothing to do with the shooting and I knew that. But these dudes ain't give two fucks they were just ready to shoot something. It was broad daylight and my homeboy walked up on dude with his gun out, the young dude wasn't trying to run but you could see the fear in his eyes. I couldn't just watch this happen so I ran up on my homeboy with the gun like hell Naw bra, you know bra ain't been with them niggas. Homeboy like ion give a fuck. I grab my homeboy and bra from Georgia just walked in his grandma house. Anyway, fast forward to like a year later. I get locked up at the age of 16. I'm reppin GD hard. They sent me to the county jail. Put me in a dorm full of Bloods. And on top of that I am in the County jail in Georgia... Niggas eyeing me crazy. I can't get no room, had to put my mat out on the Rock with the lame niggas, and the crackheads. There I was, sitting on that mat looking crazy and confused like, "How the fuck I get there?" I was out there for like an hour. Then that same l'il nigga come out his room look and see me. We locked eyes and I was like damn. Shit about to get Gangster in this Bitch. Bra walked down the steps I stood up. He extended his hand, and we shook hands. The handshake was firm with respect. Real niggas know you can tell how a nigga feel from his handshake. But yea. Bra moved me in his room with him and his homeboy. I fought plenty times in that county jail. But every time I did, bra was right there making sure I got a fair one. Moral. Of. The. Story. You never know who you might need.

A Fool With A Plan

See, I ain't no real writer but I always loved to write, and draw. I started when I was young writing poems and drawing, I was good, but eventually it faded away and I faded into other things. And shortly after I faded into the other things. I ended up fading into the prison system where I stayed for the next ten years, I was convicted of armed robbery, my first offense, first time ever being in handcuffs, only sixteen years old. I had messed, you I know I had done wrong, and I was willing to accept my consequences but damn ten years day for day. Nobody was hurt, and no real money was taken, now that really messed my life up. See I was never a thug, honestly. I was a good kid, I dressed nice I spoke well, and I was always smart. I always tried to find someone to blame for me going to prison but now I know that it was my fault. I always say man them crackers railroaded me, then I say my life at home was crazy, my family situation was crazy, I was a child that was hurt, scorn, and beat and torn. Then I think about all the other successful people that went through what I did and maybe worse.so I am done making excuses. Now we got to fast forward 14 years later. I been out of prison almost three and a half years things were different. Everything was new and big, and everything was always moving fast, like I was losing time, everybody always telling me to slow down and have patience and you're moving too fast. But I always had that feeling like I had missed out on so much that I deserved it, kind of like I was just focused on trying to catch up on all I had missed out on. Since being on the run for murder, I know I have a bad case of anxiety, depression, claustrophobic, paranoia, all that good stuff. And prison did it, it's only three things that I am scared of and that's God, Dying, and Prison. Prison is hell on earth full of war blood and hatred, it's almost no-good days, so after being out for those few years there has been good times and most definitely been bad times. I'm learning to accept the way God has things planned. So back to my story… When I got out, I moved to Greenwood S.C. It was cool, a small country town but cool. So, here's me this young black man, in a lot of trouble, and he needs God sooo Bad. He Prayed and Prayed. But deep down inside he also knew that he had to work towards what he prayed for, I told myself that I had to come up with 100,000 dollars to get myself out of this situation I was in. HOW DO YOU START FROM NOTHING AND MAKE IT TO A HUNED GEES????? God please help was my words spoken to deaf ears. I felt so bad not being able to be there for my mother who I knew needed me, I had so many answers with no questions. I needed to talk to

God, and I needed answers right then it wasn't no time to wait. I prayed for things and looked up to the sky right after praying, already disappointed asking God like why haven't you done that yet? My faith was on the fence badly, I did not see no way out. The last thing I wanted was to go back to prison, to go back to being alone, to go back to being forgotten, to go back to being an animal, and not a Human Being, those are just some of the things that prison deprives you of. Now years down the line, I think about what being on the run and being hunted did to me. It messed me up bad mentally. Now here I am at thirty-five, and I have done more years in prison than I have being an adult. I just had started to get use to showing me I.D and buying alcohol, small things to a normal person, but to me these we're things that I had dreamed about doing for so many years.

Trying

I wanted what I wanted; I gave very little but expected a lot. I looked for more, tried less and became a had not. But it is never too late to try. If you ever wake up and want to do it again the first thing you must do is believe that you can, if you have never not succeeded, most likely it is because of how hard you didn't try, hope and faith starts inside of us, not with the most high. We must want to do better for us to do better. We start, it gets hard, we stop, we hurt, we cried, we lost once, lost again. We are okay with giving up, just because we tried. Trying is when you gave your all to your all, and once you really try, you could never fail. Trying starts with wanting. Trying doesn't know I can't. I tried is the first step towards your goal. Trying is the one way to always hold on.

Love or Loyalty

Which of the two would you rather have given,

　　Love or Loyalty?

Which of the two would give you the better feeling,

　　Love or Loyalty?

Love is an emotion that sways from time to time,

Loyalty is unwavering and never draws a line.

They say that love conquers all,

But we know one thing about loyalty, and that is, it never falls,

And sometimes love do not live there anymore,

When loyalty never leaves at all.

Love dies,

And loyalty lives on.

Love hurts, while loyalty never leaves you alone,

So, which of the two is greater, Love or loyalty?

Forgiveness

Forgive me for wondering constantly whether I am forgiven, because if I knew for a fact that I was forgiven, would I feel how I feel from the very beginning?

Forgive me for my worrying my friend. Forgiveness is something that everyone does not get. Most say they forgive you but can never forget. Society tells us not to be so forgiving, so it's often so confusing.

Forgive me for asking for what I was promised, not entitled, but what I deserve. Forgiveness is an action, most definitely not just a word.

Broken

I once had a wounded heart and carried so

much anger and depression. How do I cope

with a mind that is missing a few screws?

With a heart that has forever been bruised,

with a soul that has been shaken and often confused.

How is it possible for a user to be used?

My mind deceived into thinking that

I was where I wanted and needed to be.

My eyes have repeatedly tricked me into

seeing things that really, I did not see.

My heart says one thing, but my tongue speaks another.

Then I finally realized that I was a broken brother.

I hated others because I once hated myself.

Being broken has caused me not to love myself.

Fathers Are Needed

Growing up I didn't have a dad or a father, but I had an older brother, but even though he use to whoop me and punish me, I never saw him as a father or a father figure. To be completely honest, and I'm not blaming anyone for my mistakes, I just know now that if my father and a lot more fathers would have been around and in their son's lives, things for the sons would have turned out different. I did a count inside of my dormitory, I walked around and asked a hundred inmates was their father in their lives growing up, and out of the hundred six had fathers that were actually in their life. I know that my father could've been three feet tall I would've still listened and respected him no matter what, because it's just something about his presence, something about the name Daddy Dad or father. I read in an article that a reason for how kids react to their father differently from the mother is because of the volumes or frequencies in the tone of the male voice. Whatever it is, it does something to a kid; anybody in the world can tell you something but for some reason it just sounds a lot sterner and stricter coming from your father, so imagine some of us kids doing some of the things we had done growing up, doing it in front of our fathers–those things wouldn't fly, imagine how scared we would have been coming home with bad grades or suspended? My mom knew how to deliver a good whooping, but it doesn't have the same effect, mothers whoop out of emotions and anger, dads whoop strictly out of love and discipline, most hate to whoop their kids especially their daughters, but I wanted to let myself and all the fathers and dads of the world know how important we are, just our love and discipline alone can change the outcome of our kids. Most of all our black fathers are needed. A lot of our kids are growing up resenting us, and not because of what the mother is saying about you, but behind what the kid is feeling–it's amazing how soon they learn and grown to love us fathers so quickly, so know that our expectations are so high with the kids. I have seen guys that was broke and busted, a nobody to a nobody but if you see them around their kids you would think these guys we're great kings the way their kids look up to them, but that's just a child's love for their dad–a kid knows you only get one, and from the playground to the school every kids daddy is the best daddy in the world. Crazy thing is on the inside it's still like that when a lot of us grow into adults. A lot of people are still crazy about their dad, and a lot of kids still hate their dads for not being there or leaving, not showing up to games and graduations, no birds and bees talks, no I love you's. We all got to do better at doing our part because I swear to you it's so important, we are so important, our relationship with our kids are important. We are needed in the households we are needed in our communities; no one can do our jobs better that we can. If you live in the same city as your kid and you and the mother is no longer together there is no way you should not see them more than three times a week, even if you live out of state you should always make a way to be in your kids' life. My dad drove 18-wheeler trucks and I remember him telling me a couple times that he had to come my way and he was gone come through and pick me up, I remember sitting out on the porch waiting, I remember waiting the next day, and the day after, and he never showed, then the next summer he would do it all over again, and I would sit and wait on him to never show, but the thing is, I still waited, and all kids love the same way, we are needed...

A Fatherless Father

Really man I do not care what y'all got to say,

My daddy wasn't no good to me,

But y'all expecting all this and that from me,

Naw, naw, nope,

Not having a Father in my life made me strong,

Just taught me that I had to learn all that man shit on my own,

This apple fell so close to the tree,

My son answers the phone and don't even know that it's me,

So, I guess in a Fatherless Father kind of way I'm doing great.

I forgot about birthdays just like my father taught me,

And the way you get mad for not being a good dad, I got that from you too.

I wonder did you feel the way I feel now?

Did you want to call more back then, the way I tell myself
I will call more now?

I wonder does he wait the way I waited on the front porch?

Does he love me after how I let him down?

The way that I loved you after you let me down?

Or do his ears hear my I love you's,

The way I didn't hear yours?

I wonder do he feel any emotions for me,

The way I didn't feel any for you?

I don't know his favorite color

Like you don't know mines...Still....

So, it's a spot in us that needs to be refilled, so that we
Fatherless Fathers can plug this spill,

So, it doesn't runneth over and my grandson doesn't
have to feel what his Father feels,

Because it is always there,

Even when you tell me it was not my fault, yet and still
that's exactly how I felt,

Or better yet, I must've not been good enough?

All the times I needed you when I was growing up,

You failed me, and I'm scarred for life,

Loving my child so much but still don't really know how to love him right,

I wasn't there like you wasn't there to be the first to teach him how to fight,

Yea that father and son moment that the ones with Fathers know about,

Them talks they have when no one else is around,

Those moments and talks I never got,

I get angry sometimes at you all over again,

You let a woman do your job, trying to raise a boy to a man,

I wonder what your father was like.

Was he like you, was he mean or was he nice?

I wonder do my son get jealous mad or angry when he sees his friends with their dads?

Because when I was coming up it sure did make me mad,

So, upset that I told my mama I don't have a dad.

And she would snap at me and tell me do not let her ever hear me say that.

But it is ok for her to cuss you out like a dog I never did get that,

You missed my first steps, man you ain't never been there,

I was losing at birth, then on top of that you weren't there,

You never put one smile on my face so tell me how that feel?

Hell, naw it isn't fair,

For this father to walk this Earth as if he does not care,

Because if care he did,

Care would have been showed,

You told me you were coming time and time and you never showed,

This what you planted are you ashamed of what you growed?

For way too many years

We stand Firm like Brother Malcom, Marcus Garvey,
and Chairman Fred,

Looking the oppressors in their eyes, telling them

They don't bury the scared they bury the dead.

We're breathing life into our people,

And we will not stop until all is equal,

We watched as they turned our fight for peace into a
war on one nation of people.

You concealed all kinds of brutal and inhumane most
violent acts to date,

And yet and still have the nerve to display so many
different forms of hate.

For way too many years,

Rivers created from my ancestors tears.

Generations of Black Men born inheriting too
many fears,

Generations of Black Men broken, beaten,
scarred and killed,

First through chains, slavery, and ropes

The latter by oppression, gavels, and the killings
of hope,

Not to mention the poverty, All the viruses
and the dope,

And why the only time we mean something to you is
when we Rap, sing, play ball or it's time to vote?

For way too many years,

Rivers created from my ancestors tears.

You turned our love and compassion into an
uncontrollable since of confusion and a huge
dose of anger,

Robbing us of our youthful peace and replacing it with
a strange reality and a strong sense of danger.

For way too many years,

Rivers created from my ancestors tears.

Deception

One good thought of you is all it takes to make my
heart smile,

My love for you could never run out of gas and it will
last for a lifetime of miles.

The heart doesn't know how to lie,

The mind sometimes can deceive us and the soul can be
persuaded,

The body only loves what loves it, often times leaving
the eyes to be once again mistaken, its deception
at its best.

How I felt today

Fuck pain

To hell with hurt

Fuck feelings

Bury emotions in the dirt.

Love is nothing

Friends doesn't exist

Having a heart isn't hitting on shit.

Love leaves you stranded

Feelings leave you abandoned.

Self-love is the best love

Fuck pain

To hell with hurt

Fuck feelings

Bury emotions in the dirt.

Daydreaming

For many hours I can lay still

Willing myself to replay the major events that took place earlier in my life.

I find myself redoing and correcting the areas that I felt like I could've done better or reacted differently.

No matter the time or place, I can daydream.

No matter the time or the place my daydreams are something that cannot be taken away from me

Chances and Changes

Before you get a chance, you will probably get a no.

To give someone a chance u will have to see them as new, mistakes will be made, we must keep them to a few, life is full of opportunities.

Chances do not come around that often, yet, and still after failing you must continue to get up, dust yourself off and step your game up.

Treat every chance just like it is your last,

Cherish each moment because time moves fast.

That is when you see changes.

God's Love

His words are so powerful, he spoke Let there be light,

The wages of sin are death, but through him we have eternal life.

For all have sinned and fallen short of his glory,

Only he is perfect, so we shall not worry.

There has been no other sacrifice as great as his son,

He died for our sins, for us he wore a crown of thorns.

God never promised that his children would travel an easy road,

But through our beliefs we know that he died, and he rose.

Through his death we have been sanctified,

And with his love we are justified.

With our love, and our faith we can repay the deed,

All he asks of us is just the faith the size of a mustard seed.

Through our trials and tribulations, we must put on the full armor of God,

Through our troubles and hardships, we must trust in the lord.

Never boast and brag, we must continue to be humble,

We will all slip, but we must get back up every time that we stumble.

No man can do the things that our God will do,

No person in this world will love you the way your God do.

He loves us through our ups and our downs,

When your best-friend leaves you stranded your God will forever be around.

God's Love

The Ink in My Pen

The Ink in my pen became the blood in my veins

The Ink in my pen became the voice for my pain

The Ink in my pen spoke the truth and told no lies

The Ink in my pen has been loved and despised

The Ink in my pen often, times gave me strength

The Ink in my pen became my very best friend

The Ink in my pen helped me bury my sorrow

The Ink in my pen gave me hope for a better tomorrow

The Ink in my pen brought joy and brought tears

The Ink in my pen made minutes feel like years

    The Ink in my pen

Religion

I think religion is very scary, it's like choosing the love of your life, only a hundred times more complex.

You want so badly to make the right decision, and after making that decision in the back of your mind you spend allot of time wondering, hoping and praying that you made the right choice. Then you start to fret if your God is upset with you for the thoughts that no one else can know or hear but him, so lately I've started to try my best to be Godly.

Never have I thought of myself as God, I think that a person with all of my imperfections could never come close, I think that the closest we could get is to only try and display a what would God do concept, but we must know and understand that no one in this world will ever be perfect, If the world was perfect there would be no fun.

Beautiful Black Woman

A beautiful black woman should be treated as such,

We must cherish her beauty, respect her mind and
value her touch.

She comes in different shapes and sizes, some are light
some are darker than other's

No matter the complexion they're our wives our sisters
and mothers.

They're strong, loyal, fierce and intelligent, without
those beautiful black women us as men could never be
relevant.

They're the oxygen to the earth and the water
in our sea,

A beautiful black woman gave birth to you
and also to me.

Her touch alone heals souls, heals wounds and
unbreak hearts,

She's consistent, persistent and mentally sharp.

To remove her from any situation would leave us
stranded and alone,

What good is a palace and being a King without a
Queen to your throne?

Her smile is enough to light up any room,

She's independent when she needs to be,

Loud and proud for the ones she love,

Where would mankind be without her?
Oh beautiful black woman you're a blessing
from above.

A letter to my Mother

I know over the years I've caused you much joy and so many more tears

But in this one letter I want to sum up just how I feel.

I want to take this time to express how much I really love you and manifest my feelings into words.

Lord knows I really do adore you, through the thick and thin you've stayed by my side, you have always been there, you never turned your back, and always showed me that you care.

You're forever my leading lady and always my number one. I'm blessed and forever grateful to have had you as my mom, I'm sorry for the hurt, I hope you forgive me for the pain. Me being your son is something that I would never want to change, you tried to make life as clear to me as possible when I tried to see things my way, you brought light to my darkness, made me warm when the world was so cold, the love that you gave me cloud never grow old.

Take the mask off

Different isn't always bad

Or something to be ashamed of,

Don't always try to conceal what just may be your
blessing.

So many of us worry so much about what so many
people whose opinion usually means nothing
or less to it,

We worry so much about what they say or feel, why?

When you're really being yourself and that facade is no
longer up that's when you begin to meet others who are
like you,

That's when you start to establish those true friendships
and foundations that grows into walls of loyalty.

Only when you take. Off the mask will you meet true
friends, you have to be you, accept you, and most
importantly you got to love you.

That's when you can finally love someone and have
someone really love you.

Black Girl, Black Woman, Black Queen

Black Girl, Black Woman, Black Queen

They were her and she was once them, fearful of the unknowing and at times not even knowing, forgetting herself and her self-worth, and most of all that she deserves.

Probably at times thinking that her value lies within her curves, that black girl learned to think like a black woman, then elevated into a black queen,

Then one day, some day she realized that she is, and she was always beautiful, and the woman of a Kings dream.

She was her, and her wanted better, then she begins to see with her eyes what her mind and her heart already knew, and that is beauty, and her beauty was true.

That is when she started to love the black girl that she had been, embraced the black woman that she was, and opened her heart to the black queen that she was destined to be.

That black girl had been beaten, that black woman had been held back, but the black queen became the moon to the universe, possessing powers she never knew as a black girl, what she never used as a black woman, and now owns as a black queen.

They are her, and she was them, the ultimate gift to the black king, Our foundation and our support beams.

The one living thing that can truly love unconditionally.

She gives life, taste right, loves hard and shines bright, that black girl adored us, that black woman loved us, that black queen is a part of us.

That black girl wanted love, that black woman wanted respect, but that black queen demanded it all, and all is what she deserves, because she was them, and they were her.

Black Girl, Black Woman, Black Queen

Black

Where I grew up red Roses never bloomed and the one
Violet I knew was black, always black and beautiful
and never blue,

Nothing was sweet, it's sad but true.
You would have to see it for yourself to understand
what we go through,

Poverty is the origin of our destination,

Growing up in a place where broke and hungry was a
recreation,

Mostly because many of us had accepted a false
realization,

Mentally defeated by the trials and tribulations that we
found ourselves constantly facing.

The seeds have been planted and our minds are finally
starting to sprout,

We're learning, teaching, growing and finally seeing the
end of our four hundred year old drought.

Imagine This

Us relaxing hand in hand, our energy all in tune with
our toes in the sand,
Watching our vibes surfing the clear blue waves,
Do you remember the days we said we would see
better days?
Our eyes are glued to the magnificent scene, from the
seagulls in the sky to the seashells floating to dry land.
This moment is greater than our greatest dreams,
far better than allot our grandest thoughts and more
spectacular than our imagination,
So this is the meaning of mental stimulation, spiritual
vibrations and sexual gratification?
The stars shine bright so bright that we see them even
though our eyes closed
Waiting patiently for the wind to send a light breeze
So our nose can smell and inhale, inhale then exhale the
beautiful mid-day aroma,
Peace is our ultimate destination,
We've made it this far through constant love and
dedication,

Let's slow dance to the rhythm and sound we created,
Let's walk on the foundation that we've made evolve,
What we molded and cultivated,
And laugh at all the silly humans who roam in our
realm and can't understand the things we see.
I would wrestle a tornado to share this feeling with the
one I love, and miss the feeling every time I blink.

Dear Ruby Lee

Dear, Ruby Lee

It's been a year and a half since you been gone, and every day I think about you, and even though you wouldn't want me to I hurt, some days for a few minutes some days more. I wish I could've been there when you needed me there, I hate that you had to be alone when you took your last breath, and I'm sorry, every day I get up and do my best to make you proud. I still see your big beautiful smile, and at the times I knew that I wasn't deserving of much of nothing. The look in your eyes when you looked at me–I could see a proud mother and I wondered how in the world could anyone be proud of me? I couldn't understand the amount of love that you had for me until you were gone, it's really amazing the level of hurt and pain it is to lose a mother. It's the kind of pain I wouldn't wish on anyone, and I just wanted to tell you thank you, thank you for trying your best and doing your best to show me a piece of the world, for trying to put your kids in a position where they could at least have a piece of opportunity. Back then I didn't understand a lot of the things you did, but I know that no matter what you did you love me, and that means more to me than anything. The world has gotten so crazy but I promise you that I'm doing my best to be successful and to make you proud, I'm going to make sure that I make you smile, forgive me for acting all crazy after you passed away, but I really didn't know how to take it–you were the only person in the world that would've gave a breath to me if I needed it to live, and I would have done the same for you, you were the only person in the world that would open the door for me morning noon or night. I remember waiting 20 minutes for you to get out of bed, get your walker and make it to the door, five minutes on the lock, and your big gap smile once that door swung open–no matter what time it was you were always happy to see me, and it isn't too many people in the world you could ever have such luck to meet. I miss you a lot, and I know you tell me every day to not hurt, and to keep on pushing on, and I will but I will never feel the same, my heart will never be the same, a piece of me left with you and I'm ok with that, as long as it's with you. I love you Mama.

Love always
Your Son, Shaad

From: Shaad
On Earth Still Loving you

We Cannot Breathe

So many names from George Floyd, we can even go back to Rodney King, Innocent black men beaten and abused, and we still cannot breathe.

We still thinking how these people could get away with what they do to us,

And this just isn't starting, we were forced here only to die a thousand deaths, to having to fight for a seat on the front of a bus,

For years we marched, yet and still we cannot breathe,

For years we protested, yet and still we cannot breathe.

How long are we expected to hold our breath?

How long can we go without breathing?

Our voices are not being heard, because we have no breath,

Our dollars are not looked at the same, so we have no wealth,

We can't get ahead, because they've made us be overly concerned with self,

And no matter how far you made it, you still could not breathe.

We have been held back long enough, it's our time, our time to breathe.

Is It A Such Thing
as Keeping It Too Real?

Is it certain levels of real, or different stages you go through or something like that? How much do you have to keep it real to prove that you real? And another question is how much do you keep it real, until you are keeping it too real? To the point where you no longer care about yourself or your well-being, to the point you don't care about your life? I remember when I was a teenager living in Phoenix City, AL. I had friends that didn't have it as good as I did, even though we're was far from rich I can honestly say that I was well taken care of. I may not have had the best shoes and clothes, but I had good clean clothes, a warm house with a bed, and I had food every day. A lot of my friends couldn't say the same thing: a lot of my friends were hungry every day, they wore the same clothes two sometimes three days straight, and this wasn't because they wanted to, this was because they had no choice. At fifteen and sixteen years old they didn't have nobody to wash and dry their clothes, they didn't have no one to make sure they ate every day, but me being me I wanted to be real, so I did what I could to show them some love. My mama didn't want me hanging around these guy's anyway, so she didn't allow them at her house, on her porch or in her yard. But whenever she would leave for work I would sneak them in and feed them and let them take a shower, all of that. I even got kicked out of the house behind staying out too late past my curfew, that's when I kind of knew I was too far gone. My mama never played the radio, she believed in beating the hell out you, point blank no cut on it, and she beat the hell out of me, but when I turned fifteen and started staying out past midnight, come home and the door locked. I knocked on the door, my mama would come to the door and tell me some stuff like, "Get your ass away from here, go back where you came from, knock on my door again I'm call the police on yo ass." It's funny as hell now, but I did all of that just to get kicked out and go live in a trailer with my two homeboys. My homeboy mama had gotten married, moved out and left the trailer to her son, who at seventeen had no car, no job, just a trailer, and two months later no lights. For the first month it was the bomb; we had parties and smoked weed, and had girls over almost every day. I wasn't thinking about going back home, I was having a great time, that is until real life sunk in, when they cut the lights and the water off, and we had to sleep under three blankets a piece. It sunk in once I had to break into my own mamma house just to take a hot shower, and me keeping it real. I left my mamma house everyday knowing that all I had to do to be warm and have a full belly was come home and tell my mamma sorry. But yet I chose to keep it real. I showered and went back out to live in the streets. So later down the years, after me keeping it real on so many other different occasions, I finally had to stop and ask myself when was someone going to keep it real with me? When would I meet someone to make these same sacrifices I make and willing to make? And I had to teach and learn myself that when you are the one that is always making the sacrifices, Every time, you're not the friends you're the fool, and most likely the one being used, real love and friendship is an action, not just words. So, when you are keeping it real just make sure it is going both ways, and don't find yourself trying to fit in by keeping it too real, which means don't be the crash dummy or the test dummy or the free pick or the follower. Things had gotten pretty rough for me in the streets while I was keeping it real, I was broke and hungry so I started doing what I was good at, which was stealing. I'm ashamed of the things I done back then, I broke into so many people's houses and their property. I'm really embarrassed but it's a part of my story and my growth. I stole things that meant a lot to people, I stole coins people were saving up, I stole food, and I would watch my mama ride by going to work every day. I would see the shame in her face while she tried her best not to look over there and see her son doing the exact opposite of what she wanted for him, and all I had to do was just go home and say ma I'm sorry I want to come back home, and she would've let me in right then and there no questions asked, but I chose to keep it real. After I had broken in most of the trailers in the trailer park we lived in, I was back broke, name in all kinds of stuff. I had to try my hand at selling crack, and didn't know what I was doing, I had a couple white friends that I chilled with when I wanted to smoke for free, that would send me to get the weed, and I would charge them double for doing it. But one day I made a hundred dollars off them. I told my friend I wanted to buy some rocks to sell, he sent me to this other dude— he had to be like twenty two twenty three, but he was older than me, he told me to meet him at this crackhead house and twenty minutes I gave him my first hundred dollars and watched my money walk off, me smiling not knowing that I just been got. When we met back up he handed me a match box, I opened it up and it had about seven or eight huge white rocks in it. I grew up in the hood and had seen crack in person and on the street but never sold it. So off first glance it did raise a small alarm on how much he had given me for only a hundred dollars, but nevertheless I was still happy. I went right in the crackhead house with my newfound crack dealer swagger, and maybe twenty minutes later sold my first piece of crack. I felt good about myself—I had made my first twenty dollars as a crack dealer. I left five minutes later and went and bought me two hotdogs, a bag of chips and a soda–walking back up the street with chili all over my mouth, feeling good, when out of nowhere here comes the lady I sold that twenty to. She screaming and hollering, "Give me my money back muthafucka! You done sold me that fake shit and made me fuck my pipe up give me my money." I'm looking at her like she crazy. I'm looking around trying to see who all looking, I gave her the rest of the money I had from what I just spent Man she was still mad about her pipe though. That's one of the things I remember about keeping it too real, don't let keeping it too real put you in a position of discomfort, it's ok to be the friend just don't be the fool.

Got to Listen Sometimes

It was October or November of 2010, and I was at Smith State prison, on my eighth year with a little over two years before I got out. I was doing bad. I really didn't hear from a lot of my family, I had gotten lost in the system. I really didn't think about the reality of me getting out, being a grown man, having to work and pay bills, taking care of responsibilities. For most of my adult life I was fed and housed by the state; they gave me shoes and clothes, safe to say that I was institutionalized. I was running around prison like I was happy to be there, still stealing and scamming and robbing people, staying in bullshit Aka surviving, I hate to say it but it's the truth, it's sad how much my mind was in prison, so sad that I let my release date sneak up on me. This is one of them times I should've listened but I didn't and my actions caused a lot of people to be hurt, so one day we out on the recreation field playing basketball, when next thing you know everybody stopped playing ball and started looking towards the fence. I turn around to look, all I see is two dudes throwing basketballs over the gate. I see guys grabbing balls running back inside, clean get away, but like four of the balls got stuck in between two of the gates. I overheard one of the dudes say, "Man I got a pound of tobacco and a phone for whoever go get them balls. When I heard that I was sold. I didn't have nothing, and it had been a while since I had something. So I runs over like what's up man I'll go, one of my older brothers walked over and told me that I wasn't going over that gate. He said to me, "Man sit your ass down you only got two years them people catch you out there they gone shoot yo ass and give you five more years." But just like the day I made my mind up that I was going to steal, I had made my mind up that I was going over that gate. I was getting them basketballs, and I wasn't gonna get caught. So after a short argument with my big brother, me and three more of my younger dumb comrades we're crawling up under the first gate, then the second, then I jumped over the third gate to get the balls–one more gate and I could've been free. I grabbed the balls threw them back over the gate, hopped back over, hauling ass back up under the last two gates. When I came up under the last gate all the inmates were screaming my name and clapping. Minutes later the officers come into the dorm and holler out mandatory lock down, emergency count. I'm looking crazy, because I had cut my hands up jumping those gates, and when they do count I know they were going to do a body search also. They locked us down and the Sargent and Lieutenant came in and did the body search. My roommate acted like he was taking a dump when they got to our door. I stripped down to my boxers did a full body turn hiding the inside of my hands, and got away–that's one of the times that I was nervous in prison. After they finished the count and body search they let us back out, everybody thinking it's all good, thinking we done got away–they scored weed, pills, cigarettes, liquor, everything for us to party with and take our minds away from being in prison. I walked down to the dudes room knocked on the door, they opened it up and it looked look how it did on Ching and Chong's when they had smoked out the car. I walked in and they gave me my phone and tobacco. I couldn't make it back to my room fast enough–all I could think about was getting on the chat line and smoking my cigarettes. Well, I know it sounds like we made a smooth lick, but we didn't, nothing ever goes right in the pen. The police on the next shift came in and went straight to them guys room and started tearing it up. They found the stash spot, while they was tearing the room up. A few of the Inmates in the dorm got together and ransacked the room and started beating the officers, everybody else started running in the room grabbing everything the officers had just confiscated. Man up to that point I had never saw anything like it. The officers started massing everyone, it was like a war in Sparta. Once they got control of the dorm, that's when those dirty cops did what they do best, and that's assault Inmates while they're in handcuffs. That night

I watched them beat my big brother in the head with a hammer, and I watched them beat several other inmates. I watched that happen to the same brother that told me not to jump that gate. We got locked down for a while after that, a couple of days after the riot with the officers the Tactical Squad came. The Tactical Squad is a group of maybe a hundred or more officers dressed in all black that comes and does this super shake down. They came and tore that dorm up, and in the process found that 12 dollar flip phone that I had jumped the gate and risked my life and my freedom for, the same phone that had gotten my big brother beaten with a hammer. I wanted to tell this story so you can see that we have to be better judges of situations and take five or ten minutes to really evaluate the situation, evaluate the outcomes, and add up the pros and cons. Sometimes what we want right then is not worth what we sacrifice later on.

I Was Gonna Steal

Bad choices for me started early on in my life, like the first time I decided to steal. My mom decided to just up and move from Ninety-Six South Carolina to Columbus Georgia one day. Why? I don't know, but I hated it, I hated everything about it. We went from us knowing everyone around us, from being up or down the street from someone that loved us, from my brother Pap and I sharing a very small but spacious and comfortable bedroom to us sleeping on floors and sharing beds with my two cousins that I love so dearly, but yet and still it wasn't the greatest situation. We moved into the Peabody Projects with my aunt, my mom's younger sister her two kids and boyfriend. Peabody Apartments was one of the roughest projects in Columbus back in the early nineties, it was so bad that you had to walk to the store with your whole family if nobody knew you. I learned that I was a thief at an early age don't know why or where I got it from, my first theft was when I was maybe six or seven years old, a bike I stole that my brother Pap ended up getting arrested for. Anyhow on this particular day my brother two cousins and myself walked to the store, I didn't have the first piece of money to my name and I had decided on the way to the store that I was going to steal something for myself from that store no matter what the cost was I was going to do it because I had worked my nerves up. I was nervous and I was thinking of what and how I was going to steal from this store without being caught. The store that set in the middle of the projects was owned and operated by a Chinese family, the store looked and reminded me of the store from the movie Menace to Society. I swear it was a look alike. Once we made it to the store and walked inside, I noticed that the entire Chinese family was working that day and thought to myself, 'I'ma have to be real good to get away with this,' because if you ever been a kid inside of a Chinese owned store you know how good they can watch a black kid. But I didn't care how many of them was in there I had made up my mind that I was going to steal. We entered and I head straight to the candy isle with confidence like I had money to buy whatever I wanted, with zero cents to my name snatched up two airheads and a couple jolly ranchers, bypassed putting them in my pockets and stuck them in my underwear. After positioning the candy comfortably, I headed back up to the front of the store. It's funny now how my big brother knew me so well that he looked at me and I saw in his eyes that he sensed I had done something wrong. After I had made it to the front I noticed that the middle aged Chinese man had come from behind the counter.

I saw him looking at me like he just knew I had been stealing. So, I instantly started to think of the lie I would tell my mom to get out of that ass whooping I surely had coming. That Chinese man started yelling and screaming words he had to know I couldn't understand, but I knew the words wasn't nothing nice. I looked at my brother and cousins for help but they just stood there looking at me shaking their nappy heads being no help at all. I knew then I was up shits creek. The small Chinese man walked towards me and grabbed my arm as gently as he could, and I screamed out like he tried to break my arm which still didn't get a reaction from my Big brother and two older cousins. He started to pat my pockets and when he didn't feel anything I thought for sure that I had him. Then he hit the front of my dingy underwear and heard the sound of the candy wrappers. It seemed like the whole store was quiet. I was busted, I was caught– my brilliant plan to steal was shot down! At seven years old I was banned from that Chinese store, and I most definitely got my ass tore up when I got back home. But what I remember most is the bad choice that I made on the way to that store that day, I had made up my mind knowing that stealing was wrong and that I would surely get my tale spanked good if I ever got caught stealing anything, but no matter what I had made up my mind that I was gone steal.

Show Them That You Want It

I remember when I was younger, I loved playing all sports but basketball in particular has always been my favorite, I think I'm pretty good at all sports but everyone does, my brother Pap was like my super hero growing up, he was always the fastest and the strongest at everything, he was my first coach and made sure that I was better than he was when he was my age. I was never a shy person just mostly unsure of myself at times and lacked confidence, but the talent was there. I practiced every day at basketball. I remember my brother bought me my first basketball goal. After that I gave up on all other sports and put all my time and energy into basketball I fell in love with the game. As a young kid I started in every recreation league game that I played, made the all-star team every year, I rode my bike for miles playing ball in other hoods and different parks around town, when I finally made it to the seventh grade and tried out for the team. I was so prepared–I had worked my tail off for two summers straight, I never missed one practice or a game but yet and still I played very little my seventh grade year, but I loved the game so much that it didn't really affect me. I understood that I wasn't the best player on the team and mostly I was just happy being on the team. So the summer of my eighth grade year I worked extra hard, I ran, I practiced my dribbling skills, I worked on my jump shot, and I put all of my energy into getting better. When tryouts came around I arrived early I worked harder than everyone else. I was confident that I had gotten better, but after working so hard still I didn't start that year either, I was crushed. I felt like my whole middle school career was a waste and it really did take allot out of me. But I remained quiet and played my part–I never said anything to the coaches or no one else about how I felt. I was arrested my eleventh-grade year for an arm robbery charge. I'm in the county jail awaiting trial, its maybe eight o'clock at night when the front door slides open and in walks who? My middle school basketball coach. You can imagine my facial expression. I was so shocked to see that man walking into that pod, I thought he was there to talk to us for a second until I saw that he was dressed in the same blue two piece that we all had on. My coach and I talked allot until I was moved, we talked allot about the mistakes we both had made in life, we talked allot about basketball, and I remember one day I asked him why he never started me or just gave me a real opportunity and he told me that I never showed him that I really wanted it, I never came to him and asked why wasn't I starting or why I wasn't getting more playing time. Moral to this story is closed mouths don't get fed, and don't be afraid to ask for something that you want.

The Blue Bird

Thoughts of an incarcerated mind was written by me throughout the time I spent in prison, from 2001-2012 then from 2016–currently. My reason behind putting these thoughts, poems and quotes together was to hopefully help someone else avoid the things that so many others go through. When I was thirteen or fourteen years old I never thought that I could be sentenced to fifty years let alone a life sentence, and you could, when I was seventeen. I watched a thirteen-year-old kid get sentenced to over forty years mandatory. The day I was sent to prison from the county jail, we road silently on a big white and blue school bus that was called the blue bird. I remember how all the older inmates would tell us stories about riding on the blue bird–they almost made it sound like a badge of honor. They told us stories of how to make shanks (Prison knives)they told us how to make set ups(prison meals) they told us stories that made prison seem cool–not one time do I remember any one of those guys telling anyone of us how to go to the law library to work on our cases, or how to get out and stay out. That morning it was maybe twenty-five or thirty of us that got chained and shackled to each other, all of us under twenty-one, all of us quietly thinking on the new environment we were about to be throwed into. I can tell you that being incarcerated is the closest to slavery you can get, those waist chains and handcuffs are on tight, and the shackles are squeezing around your ankles and none of those cops want to hear you complaining about them. Being too tight. That bus didn't have the same smell that the bus I rode to high school had; in high school when I got on that bus I smelled a future, when I got on that blue bird I smelled failure, I smelled pain and hurt. All of us was afraid to look each other in the eyes, we were afraid that someone would see the fear in our eyes, we were afraid that someone would see the guilt and the hurt that we held inside so good. We all had that feeling of wishing that we were anywhere in the world but there, we all knew that we had really messed up and unlike allot of mistakes we made in the past. This was one that we couldn't get ourselves out of, nobody made any jokes on that ride, nobody smiled. It was a ride with little words. We arrived at Coastal State Prison some time that afternoon. I think it was a good three hour ride. A normal person never gets use to a stranger telling him to get naked and squat and cough, but that afternoon they furthered their fight to put a dent in all of our pride; they lined us up outside in the cold and told all of us to strip down to our underwear and socks, all of our clothes were tossed into a big green garbage can, and we were told that it would be a while before we wear anything like that again so get use to what they gave us, they walked us inside of a gym like building where we were told to take everything off and we showered together ten at a time. They shaved our heads bald and throughout the entire process you could see the confusion and pain in all of our faces and demeanor–we didn't know it but the cops were breaking us. They were tearing down hundreds of young black men at one time. They told us that we weren't good enough to shower on our own and we didn't deserve a decent haircut, that we were criminals now and the scum of the earth. After another three hours of being examined by medical and filling out different forms, we finally arrived to our living quarters where only the strong would survive.

Turned out

So, the stories that I wrote about are one hundred percent truth and factual, but I cannot and will not use actual names. But that morning on that blue bird we all knew that all of us would not serve our sentences without any major problems or conflicts. It was a mixture of sheep and wolves, for some of us prison would be just another chapter in our lives and for some prison would put a dent in their lives. Like I told you, that morning on that bus no one wanted to look into the eyes of the next man because we were all afraid of what we might reveal or see. No one wanted to be looked at as scary or weak, and no one wanted to be labeled as being soft. But truth be told, prison will make the toughest man soft! Prison will also turn the softest man into a stone cold killer! All thirty of us had made a pact that we would stick together throughout our journey–we thought that we would be together, but that changed once we made it to the first building and they started splitting us up. We were all shocked! They started to put three or four in this dorm, six or seven over there, another four of five there, and there was this one young brother in particular that was sent into a dorm by himself. He was waiting for the officer to call someone else's name to go with him but the officer didn't. At that time the fear in his eyes was no longer able to be concealed, everyone could see it on his face, it was evident in his body language. He was confused to why was he the only one going into a dorm alone. We all felt bad for "Tremaine." He stood at maybe five foot seven and only a hundred and fifty pounds. He was a quiet, cool dude, sentenced to fifteen years for attempted murder and kidnapping. I know that feeling he had that day, the why me feeling. Out of all thirty names, his had to be the one that was picked to be put into a prison dorm full of people that he didn't know. We all shook his hand and told him that we gonna come check on him every day if we could. When I shook his hand it was wet with sweat. But he didn't have to be afraid by himself, we were all afraid for him. Hell, this was prison and none of us had been there before. Tremaine walked into that building by himself that day and the nine of us didn't know that that would be the last time we would see the young man that we had grown up with in the county jail. Since all of us were under twenty-one, we ate chow together three times a day, so we all embraced that time together and we never missed chow. After maybe a week we started seeing less of Tremaine, so we all started to worry about him. One day, about ten of us snuck over to the dormitory that he was placed in, we knocked on the window and told some guys to go get the light skin nigga that just came in there. His name's Tremaine; a few dudes was looking at us like they didn't know who we were talking about, and after a few minutes somebody knew who we were looking for and went to go let him know that we was at the window. It took him a couple minutes to show up, but when he did, we all stood there with fury in our eyes. Tremaine had a black eye, and was walking with a limp. We stood there in shock for a minute, finally realizing that prison was real, that our situation was real. We all asked him over and over again who had done that to him, but he kept telling us to not worry about it, that he was good. We even tried to get the officer to open up the door for us–we wanted to defend our friend, but our friend didn't want us to defend him. After a couple minutes of us just standing there sad face shaking our heads, a big black dude walked up. He was so tall and so big, he looked to be in his early forties or something like that. He came up to Tremaine and told him something, and that's when our friend told us that he had to go. To see the youthful joy that he once possessed gone, to see the big smile that he carried with him everywhere replaced with sadness and fear had done something to all our spirits. It changed us all that morning–it didn't take a rocket scientist to figure out what was going on with our friend. Ultimately, Tremaine stopped hanging and eating with us. Instead, he did everything with his

"War Daddy." (The person that takes care of protect and sleep with another man) Everywhere we saw Tremaine we would see that big tall black man. It got to the point that we all stopped talking to our friend, as he no longer wanted our help. Or friendship. I guess he had figured it out on his own.

I hope God is a Forgiving God

I Truly hope and pray that God is a forgiving God, because some of the things I've done are questionable. Sometimes I lay around and I think to myself, "Shaad, do you really think God will forgive you for hunching on that girl when y'all was in church? lol." and, "kissing all on the church van? lol." But then I think about all the times that God has reassured so many others and myself that he is a forgiving God. So, when I start being all down on myself I try my best to remember that God is a good God, and that no one in this world has ever been or will ever be perfect; that's the good thing about religion, that's the good thing about having a God it makes life easier for us all by us having something to believe in that is greater than ourselves. I know there are millions of others in the world that just want to give up sometimes because they feel like there's no coming back from some of the things they have done. Well, I'm here to tell you all that there is nothing new under the sun, and people are like a deck of cards–you never know who's who until the cards are turned over, and God is playing all the cards, so he's the only one that know who's a spade a heart diamond or club.

I Was Not Prepared

I was released from prison on January 4th 2012, ironically on my birthday. It was a cool Monday morning–no lie this is my first time experiencing feeling the feeling of something being surreal. When I was walking out of those doors with no chains or shackles on for the first time in ten years, it felt so unreal. The clothes I had on felt different, and the first thing that came to my mind was my first day in prison when that officer took all of our clothes and threw them into that thrash can and told us that it would be a long time before we felt clothes like that again. That morning when I was leaving, I could see my fellow brothers on the rec field, and I could see the smiles on their faces from where I was. I could even feel their smiles, they were happy to see one of their own leaving that place. I gave them hope! They saw me going home after ten years, which made them feel closer to home. The more I looked over at them over my shoulders the sadder I became. I wanted to take all of them with me. I knew it was dudes that I was leaving behind that had committed lesser crimes than I had committed and some were even innocent, some had been there longer than myself. I wanted to free all of them! It finally hit me that I was really free once I walked through those last two security gates. It seemed as if the sun had started to shine on me once my feet had hit that parking lot. I know there are a lot of great feelings in the world, but I could almost compare one getting out of prison to a slave that was freed after years of enslavement. I wasn't in no rush to get off of that property–I just wanted to cherish the thought and the fact that I could do whatever I wanted to do that day, the thought that no one could tell me to stand up or to walk in a straight line or how long I had to finishing eating. I had something back that had been taken away from me, something that when you don't have it you're not living, and that's my freedom! How could a man be a man without his freedom? When you're not free you don't have any rights, you don't have the freedom to go and come as you please, you don't have your freedom of speech. I was so excited that day, it was the first time that I had been happy since the time I had seen my mom after all those years. Finally, my smile wasn't forced, finally I didn't have to look and act so tough and so mean, finally I could actually love and respect people for who they were again. The sad thing about me getting out of prison after serving ten years was that after a week of being released. I realized one day that I wasn't prepared, that's when I started to beat myself up for being so stupid. I realized that I had sat in prison for ten years and failed to earn a free education, that I had failed to earn any degrees, that I had failed to learn a trade. That's when the harsh reality hit me that I wasn't ready. I didn't know what to do or where to start, which put me in a position to fail, which ultimately lead to me being where I am now, back in prison for murder with fifteen more years to serve. Proper preparations prevent poor performances.

My Biggest Disappointment

Growing up, I'm willing to bet anything that my mom expected nothing short of greatness from me. She was a real disciplinarian, and I don't think my dad would have been as strict on me then she was. She really didn't play the radio with me–I was bad but I wasn't disrespectful so I only got in trouble for the normal things that young boys my age would get into. My grades were average all through school, and I wasn't a bad student. That's just something my mother wouldn't had tolerated; my mom was from the old school, she didn't believe in parents being friends with their children around our house it was all work no play and kids didn't mingle with grown folk, education was number one in our house. My mother went back to school and got her G.E.D when she was in her forties, which was one of the most jubilant days of her life. We had our differences when I started to get older but still it wasn't a concern. I was the baby boy. Neither of her older two sons had ever been in trouble with the law and both of them had graduated from high school and without a shadow of a doubt she really thought I would also. At the age of fifteen things took a turn for the worse for us, the whoopings that she was a MVP at wasn't doing enough for me which surprised her. I started running away and staying out all times of night. I had other family members that loved me dearly and would have gladly took me in, but my momma was a proud woman and I think she didn't want to admit that at some point and time, she had went wrong somewhere with me. So, she soon had washed her hands with me. She called me in her room one day and told me that she had had a dream and God had told her to let go and that he had me. After that she just kind of let me do what I wanted to do, and at sixteen years old I was living life like a grown man. I think that after I was locked up she felt that it was her fault, which it wasn't. I think that we both played a part in me being behind bars at such a young age, but most definitely more of my fault than hers. After serving ten years and getting out seeing my mom's condition wasn't so good, I felt that I owed it to her to take good care of her the way she had done for me. So, I cooked for her, I cleaned for her, I made sure she took her medication, and I washed her. I felt that it was my fault for the stress I put on her which was the cause of her suffering from all those strokes she had. My biggest disappointment in life was when I was arrested for murder four years after being released from serving a ten year bid. I had let her down. I know that I was all she had. I watched her go downhill from home and prison. I watched her be mistreated and be unloved and unappreciated, and I watched her give up. My mom passed away on Feb 27, 2019,alone in a nursing home, not surrounded by any loved ones, not with anyone that cared. I remember my first cousin calling me. When I answered the phone, I felt it in my heart; he could barely get the words out, but I knew, my heart felt it first. So, me not being there for her when she needed me the most was the biggest disappointment of my life.